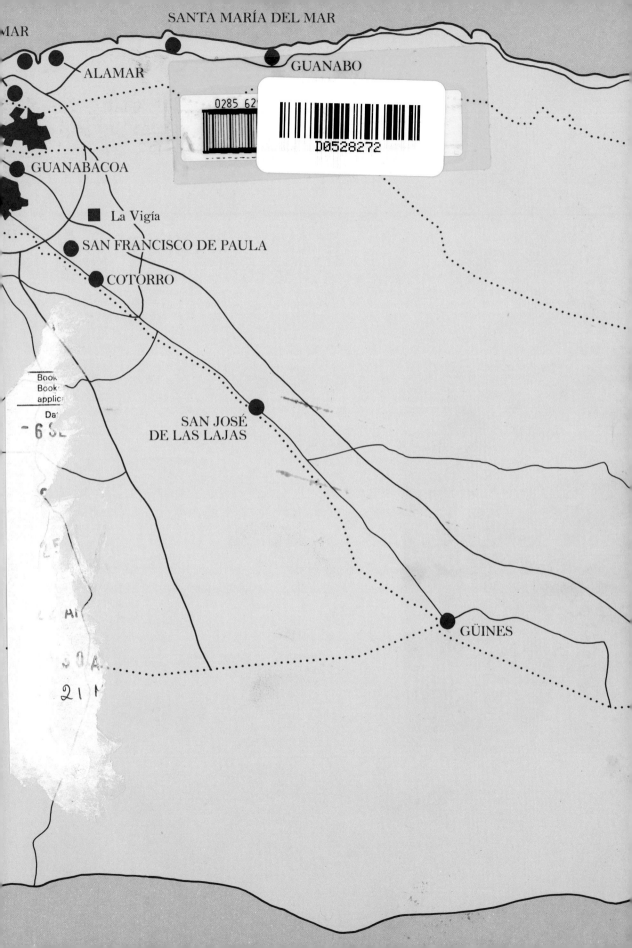

SIX DAYS IN HAVANA

SIX DAYS IN HAVANA

by James A. Michener
and John Kings

SOUVENIR PRESS

Copyright © 1989 by James A. Michener
and John Kings
All rights reserved
Printed and bound in Japan

First British Edition published 1990
by Souvenir Press Ltd.
43 Great Russell Street,
London WC1B 3PA

ISBN 0-285-62959-X

LEABHARLANNA ATHA CLIATH
DOLPHIN'S BARN LIBRARY
ACC. NO.   0285 62959X
COPY NO.   ZZ 1004
INV NO/91 1718
PRICE IR£   17.78
CLASS   917.291

James A. Michener and John Kings
gratefully acknowledge research and
photographic assistance extended by the
United States Information Agency,
Havana, Cuba.

The photographs on pages 6–16
are reproduced courtesy of
The Special Collections
University of Miami Library,
Coral Gables, Florida.

BOOKS BY
JAMES A. MICHENER

Tales of the South Pacific
The Fires of Spring
Return to Paradise
The Voice of Asia
The Bridges at Toko-Ri
Sayonara
The Floating World
The Bridge at Andau
Hawaii
Report of the County Chairman
Caravans
The Source
Iberia
Presidential Lottery
The Quality of Life
Kent State: What Happened and Why
The Drifters
A Michener Miscellany: 1950–1970
Centennial
Sports in America
Chesapeake
The Covenant
Space
Poland
Texas
Legacy
Alaska
Journey

with A. Grove Day
Rascals in Paradise

BY
JOHN KINGS

In Search of Centennial

Contents

HAVANA BOUND   7
by John Kings

IMAGES   17
by James A. Michener
  First Impressions   26
  Roaming Havana   43
  Finding My House in El Cerro   69
  Placid Experiences   77
  Coffee or Sugar?   85

IN HAVANA   95
by John Kings
  The Old City   102
  The Gilded Age   109
  Faded Glory   116
  Street Life Today   125
  Cubans   131
  America in Cuba   138

Havana Bound

Brainse Carrran Cloch
Dolphin's Barn Branch
Tel: 540681

by John Kings

WHEN JAMES MICHENER, with whom I work, decided to turn his attention to a long novel on the Caribbean I began to collect background information that might be relevant to his research. Over the years he had made repeated trips to most of the islands, to many of them several times, but was not conversant with the main French islands of Martinique and Guadeloupe, nor had he ever been to Cuba or Jamaica. I knew the French islands moderately well, the British not at all, and I, too, had never visited either Cuba or Jamaica. Within a few months of moving to Miami as a base for his research and writing, Michener had rectified both the French omissions and the Jamaican but still had not been able, because of political restraints, to visit Cuba, perhaps the most important Caribbean island, certainly the largest and closest to the United States.

Before the visit to Cuba that led to the preparation of this book, my knowledge and awareness of the island and of its capital, Havana, were deplorably hazy. When I lived in London, my experience of that far-away island was limited to the occasional smoking of an expensive *Romeo & Juliet* cigar and to enjoying the cinematic adventures of Alec Guiness, Ralph Richardson, and Noel Coward in Graham Greene's *Our Man in Havana*. These diversions, educative though they were in a sense, hardly constituted a well-rounded appraisal of either Cuba or Cubans. For the rest, my vision was limited to a vague recollection that Theodore Roosevelt had led a dashing cavalry charge up San Juan Hill, though exactly to what end I did not know, and that

the battleship *Maine* foundered in Havana bay. And, by some quirk of previous research undertaken at the Buffalo Bill Historical Center in Cody, Wyoming, I knew that artist Frederic Remington was also present in Cuba, recording the exploits of Teddy and the U.S. Cavalry with his unequaled equine sketches. Finally, I was, of course, aware of the United States' debacle of the Bay of Pigs, and after living for the past two years in Miami I was well aware of the views of our immigrant Cubans.

Clearly there was room to improve my knowledge of Cuba and of many other islands whose Spanish, English, French, or Dutch history was equally blurry in my mind. Perhaps Americans as well as Europeans tend to think of the Caribbean as a single entity largely comprised of coconut palms and golden sands; that one reaches it easily by air

and returns with a tan and a couple of bottles of
duty-free rum. If this is so, I was not alone in my
lack of knowledge and I needed the clarification of a
Michener novel on the area to help me understand
the enormous cultural differences and vicissitudes of
history that had contributed to the cauldron loosely
termed the Caribbean. With its three main European languages, a half-dozen colonial powers jock-
eying for control of the fabled islands over a period
of five hundred years, and the whole mosaic overlaid
with a predominantly African and to a lesser extent
East Indian heritage, not to mention the original
ethnic Caribbean peoples, there was obviously room
for research and reflection, and it would surprise no
one that James Michener was striving to identify
and explain these richly contrasting factors within
the covers of one long novel.

My first move, preparatory to actual journeys in
the Caribbean, was to ask the tourist office of each
island government in the region to send its normal
package of information. I was soon bombarded with
brochures that listed many of the contacts and
phone numbers I needed to begin planning the
many research trips in which Michener would criss-
cross the Caribbean during the next two and a half
years. The brochures also gave me a rich variety of
historic, economic, and geographic material. The
tendency was for the larger islands to send the least
general information and to include the brochures of
every large resort hotel, the smaller islands to herald
their importance in effusive and creative prose.
From all of it two facts became abundantly clear.
First, that Christopher Columbus had personally
discovered each and every island and, second, that
Eden itself exists in all of them.

And what of Cuba? The Cuban Tourist Office in
Montreal, probably thinking I was a Canadian so-
journing in Miami, sent an average pack of basic
information, somewhat distorting the course of history and concentrating on beach resorts in various
parts of the island. The statement that 'in 1898
Spain and the United States signed the Treaty of
Paris by which Cuba was handed over to the United
States—a blow that once again dashed the Cubans'
hopes of independence—seemed to call for verifica-
tion, but it did serve to rekindle my interest in San
Juan Hill and Teddy Roosevelt.

When it became apparent that we would finally
get to Cuba I looked for ways to improve my knowledge, and since contemporary photographic refer-
ence on Cuba is not easy to find in the United States
I decided to see what was available from the past.
Where better to look for such material than in the
photographic archives at the University of Miami?
For two years we had been using the resources of

the library extensively and successfully. Now, perhaps, I would also be lucky in my search for photographic material. In the Special Collections I found a treasure trove of old photographs, mostly from the turn of the century, and the images could not have been stronger in evoking a sense of colonial despotism, and elegance and wealth, and poverty, grandeur, and despair. I might not yet know how to assess modern Cuba, but after looking through the pages of long-forgotten albums I most surely could sense where it had come from. So vivid was the evidence of life in Havana around the time of its independence from Spain that I could almost smell the musty odors of the streets, join in the innocent pastimes of the privileged class, and share the despera-

tion of the poor. So gripping were the images and scenes that I must share some of them with you now. In a sense they became the thermometer by which I was to gauge the temperature of life in Havana today.

The most obvious finding, and perhaps the most to be expected, was that Cuba was an elitist Spanish colonial society of white over black, rich over poor. Little wonder that photographs of a later period boasted shot after shot of a fine statue of Cuba's revered hero of liberation, José Martí. My biggest surprise was finding an album of photographs of the four-month Spanish-American War of 1898. Even San Juan Hill was shown, and one cavalry officer mounted on a white charger must surely be Teddy Roosevelt himself, although the caption states merely '1st Battalion, 2nd Maine Regiment.'

In Barbados, Jamaica, and Trinidad, Michener and I had sought the flavor of the colonial past, but nothing we found matched the messages of those Cuban albums. Perhaps the relatively small size of the cities in the other islands had made me quite unprepared for the majestic architectural sweep of Havana as shown in those old photographs. Neither Kingston, Jamaica, nor Port-of-Spain, Trinidad, nor certainly Bridgetown, Barbados, had ever looked so grand as 'La Habana,' Cuba. They were essentially provincial towns, whereas it was obvious that Havana had once been an international city of great beauty.

The question now remaining was: How would we find Cuba today, ninety years after Spain's domination, thirty years after Castro's coup, thirty years into the reported bleakness of a communist regime, thirty years into the rhetoric of hate between Cuba and the United States? With a sense almost of resignation, and at best muted expectancy, we left Miami to bring the old photographs up to date.

"The wine may be bitter,
but it's ours."
—JOSÉ MARTÍ

Images

by James A. Michener

Images

IT WAS AGGRAVATING. I was finishing a novel about the Caribbean and had visited every island involved in the plot but one, most of them several times: Barbados on the east to Cozumel on the west, including the former Danish Virgin Islands in the north and Dutch Curaçao on the south. The one I had missed was Cuba, most important of all, and it seemed there would be no way for me to get there.

The tactical situation was this: because Fidel Castro had turned the island into a communist bastion in league with the Soviet Union, relations with the United States had been severed. Our State Department would not allow me to visit Havana, and Cuba would look at me with suspicion since I was a writer who might report unfavorably on the revolution. So I was blocked at both ends of the brief flight from Miami to Havana.

For two years I had tried sporadically to worm my way into Cuba, but found myself in a cat-and-mouse situation: when the Cubans said they would allow me in, the Americans said no and vice versa. Our government is rigid in permitting no tourism, because tourists spend dollars and since Cuba's leaders had announced, after the Bay of Pigs fiasco and the missile crisis, that they were mortal enemies of the United States, a fiercely efficient trade embargo had been enforced.

It was obligatory that I include a chapter on Cuba, for it was the major nation in the Caribbean, and since I couldn't get there, I did what many writers have done in the past: I studied all available material relevant to the particular story I wanted to tell and I suppose I read fifty books and major articles

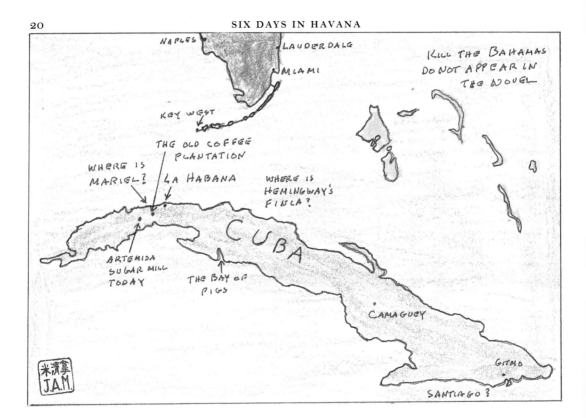

about the three decades 1958–1988. Since the Cuban passages in my manuscript dealt with locations I had been unable to visit, I drew maps to familiarize myself with the territory, memorized the residential areas and important streets, and held discussions with people who had fled Castro and were now living in Miami. At the end of this concentrated research, I was prepared to write as effectively as one could without actually wandering through the city.

But two painful gaps remained. I could not visualize the house in which my Havana couple lived, nor did anything I read enable me to construct a clear picture of their sugar plantation. I was immobilized by the lack of a house and a sugar finca and I vowed: 'Somehow I'm going to slip into Havana.'

I discover new facts about Cuba.   Retreating to my books and transferring to Cuba understandings I had acquired while working on other nearby islands, I came upon several surprising facts that might otherwise have escaped me. Repeatedly, in the literature dealing with the years 1650 through 1950 I came upon statements like this: 'At the height of this rebellion the wealthier and better-educated Spanish families, those who could escape, crowded into their boats and fled to Cuba.' This meant that through the centuries Cuba had received a constant infusion of the most energetic Spanish people in the Caribbean.

Understandably, those who escaped rebellion in Jamaica or Haiti or Santo Domingo did not want to experience another in Cuba, so the Spaniards there became increasingly conservative. This meant that Cuba was the last territory in North America to abolish slavery, in 1886, and the last by a large margin to overthrow Spanish dictatorship, in 1898. The Cuban Spanish were a tough, able, unique group, one of the strongest cultural stocks in the New World.

I learned of the strong desire among certain Cuban patriots, in the 1898–1910 period following independence from Spain, to join the United States, and the persistence of that yearning through the years. Historical accidents, some stupid, some regrettable, prevented the union but did not quench a symbiotic relationship between the two nations.

Finally, it seemed clear that by the 1950s well-to-do American businessmen and tourists were using Cuba for their own interests, the former as a source for easy profits in sugar, the latter as a kind of joyous bordello.

I needed this background material but I did not intend using it. My story would involve only the summer of 1988 when members of a conservative Cuban exile family living happily in Miami would visit their once-intimate liberal relatives living with equal happiness in Havana. I drafted my chapter in minute detail, developed a perceptive relationship between the two married couples in their late forties, and had what I believed to be a fine solid account. But it had one terrible weakness: I could not

visualize what kind of house my Havana couple occupied or how their family sugar plantation had
been organized. In other words, I suffered from a
weakness fatal to a writer: I could not evoke the
imagery I needed to make my story sing with the
required authenticity. I was sure I could mask my
deficiency from my readers, for my research was
thorough, but I could not hide it from myself.

Why visiting Havana was inescapable. Although I desperately wanted to visit Havana, my target remained extremely limited: a house and a plantation. I did not want to visit all of Cuba, nor probe its
political structure, nor meet with its rulers or its dissi-
dents, nor do the things I would normally do when
trying to comprehend a completely alien society.

In applying for a visa I had two factors in my favor,
one against. My book *Iberia,* an account of Hispanic
culture and achievements, had been enthusiastically
accepted in Spanish circles throughout the world as a
just evaluation of their societies. And I was known as a
writer who did not bring his typewriter as a stiletto
with which to skewer unfamiliar things. Foreign nations, by and large, had welcomed me and I expected
Cuba to do the same. There was every reason for the
United States to allow me to go.

The drawback was that I had been for five years a
member of the board that supervises our nation's overseas broadcasts to foreign countries, the United States
Information Agency, and was currently a member of
the powerful board that actually ran our two broadcast
services to nations behind the Iron Curtain, Radio
Free Europe and Radio Liberty. This obviously meant
that I was involved in the cold war against Communism, but of course my books on the Hungarian Revolution of 1956 and on Poland through the centuries
had amply demonstrated that. There was every reason
for Communist Cuba to keep me out.

My fairy-tale flight to Cuba. In midsummer 1988, the period in which my story took place, word came through from both governments that I would be allowed to visit Havana, briefly but without my wife, who was forbidden because she would have to be considered a tourist whose spending would give the Cubans much-needed dollars.

Several times each week, at one o'clock in the morning when the fewest casual wanderers through the airport would be aware of the fact, planes leave Miami for Havana, the shadowy process imitating scenes from Franz Kafka. I waited in line for an hour and forty minutes with no one able to explain the delay, and at last my papers were checked by an efficient young woman and I was escorted with maximum security and mysteriousness to the waiting plane.

The staggering fact about this clandestine midnight excursion is this: the flight from Miami to Havana, two of the major cities of the New World, required exactly thirty-eight minutes. Planes between the two cities ought to be operating like a shuttle, every two hours from six in the morning till midnight with ticket sales automatic and the only paperwork required a valid passport. That such interchange has been forbidden is an international tragedy.

During the brief flight I framed the two-part logic that justified my visit: 'If President Reagan, the world's prototypical anti-communist, can travel thousands of miles to visit Russia and embrace Gorbachev in the shadow of the Kremlin, I ought to be allowed to fly ninety miles to visit a house and sugar mill in Cuba.' And: 'Although it sounds silly to visit a city as dramatic and varied as Havana for only six days, I'm not some starry-eyed novice. I've spent my life visiting strange lands and grasping for understandings. In six of my customary work days, eighteen hours each, I ought to be able to locate and study a house and a plantation.'

First Impressions

SINCE I HAD LABORED so diligently to get into Cuba and since my visit was so important to my writing, I was predisposed to ignore minor inconveniences: 'You wanted to be here,' I told myself, 'and here you are. So keep your mouth shut.' But even so, my reception started disastrously.

At Immigration a surly young man treated me with such animosity that I seriously feared I was going to be sent back on the return plane, for he scowled at me, spoke only in muffled Spanish, and refused to listen to my explanations, awkwardly expressed in his language, for although I spoke Spanish, my vocabulary was limited to schoolroom phrases.

The problem was this: 'You cannot enter Cuba unless you have a known place to stay and have paid for it in advance. No gypsies welcome, no beachcombers.' Because of the highly informal nature of my visit, I had made no such arrangements. At three o'clock in the morning in an inhospitable airport, prospects were not bright.

Then came a cheery voice from the other side of the barrier: 'Michener! All's well! Everything's arranged! I'll explain to the man!' The cry came from a feisty, bearded young redhead who would be my guide and mentor during my stay in Havana, and with a reassuring skill mastered during many such midnight catastrophes, he explained conditions to the Immigration officer, jollied him along, established my credentials, and whisked me past the barrier. As I left, the Immigration officer threw me a salute, which I acknowledged with a polite nod.

My savior was Jerry Scott, public affairs officer at the tiny American Diplomatic Mission representing U.S. interests in Cuba in the absence of formal embassy ties. He was an enthusiastic man with years of service in the various nations of Latin America and ideally suited to his present job in that he respected Hispanic culture, was trusted by Cubans with whom he met daily, but remained fiercely and openly protective of our own national interests. He was aided in his work by the fact that when serving our embassy in Argentina he had married Patricia Sonschein, a beautiful, witty young woman of that country who now worked beside him as refugee coordinator taking care of ex-political prisoners hoping to emigrate to Miami.

On this night Jerry proved ultra-efficient even though I lacked a named hotel in which to stay. As dawn approached, he plopped me into his car and we headed toward Havana, the city I had so longed to see and for such a long time.

Now everything turned propitious, for it was a beautiful starlit night, and I approached the outskirts of the city in almost ideal conditions, with Jerry at my elbow explaining what areas we were traversing. As I twisted my head excitedly from side to side, I expected to see the kind of Hispanic city with which I had become so familiar during my protracted residences in Spain, Mexico, and South Texas.

What a shock! 'My God! This city needs ten million dollars' worth of white paint!' for the houses and business places in that part of town were so decrepit in appearance that anyone who loved cities would have to protest. It was not one house or building that was devoid of paint; it was entire streets, almost whole districts; proof that a beautiful city was wearing away was inescapable.

My next shock came when we left what had been essentially a business district and entered upon a chain of streets containing private houses with lawns, but since none of the householders had access to mowers, the grass grew wild, almost obscuring the residences behind. No family with even a glimmer of pride would want to live in such a setting; every inclination would be to get out and chop down that offending grass, but when there were no aids to help, the householders obviously said: 'To hell with it.'

Slumped in the car I mumbled: 'White paint and lawnmowers! With all the reading I've done how could I possibly have deduced that those were the shortages that would strike my eye?'

Then Scott said: 'Now comes the lovely part, the Malecón,' and he slowed the car as we took a long swing to double back upon a handsome boulevard edging the ocean with a broad walkway for pedestrians. Even though it was hours before dawn, two pairs of young people were strolling along, and he said: 'On the Malecón there are always lovers,' and during the days that followed, as I made many trips back and forth at all hours, I found this to be true.

Toward the western end of the Malecón, which ran for what seemed like two miles, making it one of the loveliest oceanfront promenades in the New World, we came upon a huge, forbidding modern building which symbolized the insanity of current conditions. It was the former United States embassy, now in possession of the Swiss, who assist a handful of low-profile American diplomats to serve there inconspicuously as the American Interests Section. The team is extremely busy, actually, handling the visa requests from Cubans who want either to visit Miami or to track relatives who have sought asylum there. I was told: 'If emigration into the United States was allowed, a flood of Cubans would flee this island.' Of course, in Washington the

Czech Embassy provided a similar section staffed by Cubans to handle the interests of their nation.

The good roads. One thing impressed me during this first ride through Havana, and would continue to do so throughout my stay: Perhaps I was lucky but not a single road I saw, and I traveled incessantly and in all directions, showed potholes and general deterioration. The roads were far superior to those with which I was familiar in other Caribbean islands and in some dozen different American states, but I never saw anyone working on them. Once when I commented on this, an American expert pointed out four facts: 'Cuban roads enjoy two tremendous advantages. They don't have to carry the immense number of cars American roads do, and they never heave up and down in winter from

being frozen. But they do suffer two real disadvantages. Tropical rains can destroy the edges of the highway, and the furious growth of vegetation attacks them constantly.' But the fact remained that someone cared about Cuba's roads and kept them almost free of potholes, at least in the areas I traveled.

Dawn was approaching when we passed through an area similar to the wealthier suburbs of any American city. It was called Vedado and had strings of houses that were inviting, with never a decrepit, unpainted wreck among them or an unmowed lawn. This was obviously Havana at its middle-class best, upper-middle perhaps, and once when I saw a fine-looking house in which lights were beginning to show, my heart caught with a thought that would haunt me during the days that followed: 'The people

in that house, if they saved their money, ought to be able to ride out to the airport and catch a plane to Atlanta or New York for a six-day holiday and do what restrained shopping they could afford and fly back home.' It is the banning of those comforting things people normally do that grieves me when I try to understand a dictatorial society.

The mournful mansions of Cubanacán. We now passed into the western space called Cubanacán, where the residences were so luxurious that they would have to be called mansions, beautifully tended, and just as I was about to ask: 'Who owns these?' Scott said: 'Embassy Row,' and it was as fine as any I had seen elsewhere, for out of pride the foreign governments kept their places immaculate, with the lawns as neatly trimmed as they would be at their embassies in Paris or Madrid.

But I had barely stopped admiring this display of
handsome architecture when we passed into the part
of Cubanacán that contained a continuation of the
grand homes, but this time not under foreign owner-
ship, and I have rarely seen a more forlorn sight. Here
were homes of 1940 and 1950 grandeur, homes on
which well-to-do Cuban businessmen and foreign visi-
tors had spent millions, and they were being allowed
to fall into slow but relentless ruin. 'It's like an Arthur
Rackham painting,' I said, 'of a country in which a
cruel king has laid waste the mansions of his enemies.'
Aghast at what I was seeing I asked Scott: 'What's
this?' and he gave a succinct reply: 'Come the revolution in 1959, these homes were all expropriated, when
the owners either fled or were kicked out of the country. At first the new regime gave the fine houses to
party officials, but that caused trouble. The officials
had to steal to maintain the houses, and when they
were seen living so high and mighty the peasants became bitter.'

'But they could have allowed ordinary people to live
in them? Four families, six to a mansion?'

'They tried that . . . in that big one over there . . .
the peasants quickly made a slum. So they stopped
that, too. But the one that looks fairly good, it's a
government office so no one complains.'

'The others?'

'You can see. No one cuts the grass. No one tends
the place. Animals creep in and year by year things
rot away.'

These mournful mansions of Cubanacán haunted
me, for in an ordinary society they would have been
put to a score of alternate uses—schools, monas-
teries, orphanages, meeting halls—but in Cuba no
workable arrangements could be devised. Said one
man: 'Everyone has a plan for using them, but no
one a way to finance them. So maybe a hundred million dollars' worth of property sinks into ruin.'

The American Residency. I must explain our living arrangements. With me was my associate John Kings, an Englishman, scholar, and editor, who had worked with me on various projects and who now supervised my office in Miami. He had the advantage of looking like several different distinguished London movie actors, Alistair Sim in particular, and he was greeted warmly wherever we moved. He had arranged our visas and had tried without much success to find a place for us to stay in Havana, but in the end the chief of our United States mission extended a personal invitation for us to stay as his guests, so toward five in the morning our tour through Havana ended at the heavily guarded gate of the U.S. Residency. It stood in the heart of Cubanacán surrounded by ruined mansions, which made its immaculate and spacious grounds even more impressive. It was a grand house of stately design, many elegant rooms, extensive gardens, and at the end of a long promenade a magnificent carved eagle spreading his protective wings. The eagle had been brought to this resting place after having been dismantled from an earlier public memorial.

The Residency was occupied by a long-time professional diplomat, John J. Taylor and his wife,
Betsy, whose son John interested me in that he had
recently published a first-rate book on the rape of
the Walt Disney empire. Jay Taylor, a practiced ne-
gotiator with previous tours in China and South
Africa, had been entrusted with a most difficult
three-pronged task: he must represent the long-
term interests of the United States, he must keep in
intimate contact with Castro's communist government, and above all he must keep the exiled Cubans
in Miami happy. The last obligation was the most
difficult, for even the slightest move he might make
to re-establish diplomatic relations with Cuba would
be interpreted by the Miami Cubans as a betrayal of
their long-range interests in overthrowing the dic-
tator. Taylor performed his tasks brilliantly and
with grace, for after protracted conversations with
him over the dining table and in his study I could
detect not the slightest deviation from his three
commissions. He represented his government's po-
sitions firmly; he entertained scores of influential
Cubans, giving them hope that relations with the
United States would not worsen; and he was metic-
ulous in defending the interests and the claims of
the Miami exiles. I was not only happy living with
the Taylors in their mansion but also rewarded by
being able to watch a professional foreign service
diplomat in action.

Once, recalling the sentimental operatic aria from
Balfe's *The Bohemian Girl,* in which the supposed
gypsy girl sings of her vaguely remembered noble
childhood, 'I dreamt I dwelt in marble halls,' I asked
the Taylors: 'And what will you do when you have
to leave these marble halls and return to your log
cabin in Tennessee?' and he said: 'The life of a diplomat is to leave one marbled hall after another, always aware that he is heading back to the log cabin.'

I was reassured when Taylor told me: 'We've arranged for Scott to show you around our city,' for I had learned that young Scott was what Americans call admiringly 'a take-charge guy,' but the two men were surprised when I explained: 'I've come to Havana to see only two things. Some houses and streets, and a sugar mill.' They laughed and promised me: 'You'll see a great deal more than that,' but I think they were relieved to learn that I had not come to complicate their lives with some contentious political agenda. The Taylors had drinks and cookies awaiting us and by the time I went to bed it was dawn. I did not fall easily to sleep for I was worrying about those abandoned mansions engulfed by weeds.

Roaming Havana

BY MIDDAY NEXT MORNING I was deep into an exploration of Old Havana with a delightful guide, the white-haired, white-bearded Cuban poet and novelist Pablo Armando Fernández, who understood my curious mission and was eager to help me complete it. As I start to report my experiences with him I must make one thing clear: never once during my entire stay in Havana did I visit any place where arrangements had been made in advance to aid me in my work or to show me something the Cuban government wanted me to see. The one thing the Cuban government did want me to see was the monstrous, well-painted billboard on the Malecón directly facing the U.S. Interests Section building. It showed a fanatical Uncle Sam growling a menace at an honest Cuban worker armed with a rifle: 'Señores Imperialistas. We have absolutely no fear!' An American staffer told me: 'The sign may be amusing but it does demonstrate how many Cubans think.'

But this was the only government interference I encountered, and as I have done in every country I have ever visited, especially Russia and China, I drove along streets that I chose on the spur of the moment and asked the driver to stop at whatever sight interested me. I then introduced myself as an American visitor interested in things Cuban and asked permission to look around. I probed into everything, asked every question that seemed sensible, and within a few minutes had the Cubans involved wanting to show me far more than I asked about in the first place. I was met with unfailing courtesy and with not a single rebuff except at a church-museum affair where the floor was being sanded: 'Come back in an hour. We'd love to visit with you,' but by then I was long gone.

No policeman ever warned me away, no soldiers were evident, I met not a single Russian, although many were in Cuba. I had the freest hand imaginable and was met with the warmest courtesies; in fact, time and again working people I met let me know that they thought of Americans like me as their friends and hoped that our countries too might soon again be friends. How many Cubans did I meet during these six jam-packed days? Perhaps two hundred, all told. From what different walks of life? From one of the highest dignitaries in the Catholic church to leading newsmen to workmen in the fields. I experienced not a single unpleasant incident, even though I was sometimes insistent almost to the point of discourtesy upon looking into things. 'Prensa norteamericano. Un amigo de Cuba con un gran interés en las cosas cubanas.' That statement that I was interested in all things Cuban opened doors.

So what did I see? I had read several stories about a little church of no special significance but of considerable interest in the life of old Havana, Iglesia de

Paula on the waterfront. Stopping there without prior notice, I found that it had long been abandoned as a church and was now headquarters for a study of popular Cuban music, a kind of little museum with scores of oversize photographs and several large oil paintings of bands of the early 1900s. From my conversations with the amiable people running the bizarre place I learned something about what had happened to religion in Cuba.

At a more formal museum at which I stopped arbitrarily, I was informed by a most gracious young woman that the place was closed that day, but when I explained my desire to see the furnishings of a house such as my imaginary characters might have occupied, she became actively interested in my project and halted her work to show me around one of those softly stated collections of domestic life which evoke past centuries. John Kings, photographing the little museum, caught her in the sunlight as she explained something to the poet Fernández, who had accompanied us, and her pose was so poetic, so exactly right, that she can serve as a portrait of all the people who were so good to me.

Casual wandering can produce unexpected de-
lights, and one day as we traveled with an architectural expert, Professor Lisandro Otero, and were
driving through a depressed area I cried: 'Whoa!
Look at that gem!' and I jumped out to announce
myself to some startled nuns who ran a retirement
home for elderly people.

They invited us in, and I could see that much love
had been spent here, for the halls sparkled from constant cleansing, the rooms were impeccable, and the

little patio was a flowering garden. Two days later I would return to this enchanted haven in a rough city to hear one of the nuns tell the history of her place: 'Built by a commoner who amassed a fortune in the tobacco industry. Bought himself a title, Count of This or That, which allowed him to place at his entrance the revered symbols proclaiming that a nobleman lived within, two flanking stone lions. When his neighbors, proper grandees of Spain with famous names, saw his lions they were outraged: "If that upstart can buy his, we don't want ours," and in protest they all took theirs down. "La Muerte de los Leones" someone called it.' Now her home boasted the only lions on the dying street, and to me they looked quite proper.

When I asked my new guide, who for obvious reasons had best not be identified: 'If a religion is outlawed, especially that of the Catholic church, how can nuns run a refuge?' He whispered: 'Did you notice that although they were eager to show you the good work they were performing they refused to be photographed? That tells everything, for the government says: "Do your good works but do them in secret. Keep a profile so low that we don't have to see you." And that's what the Church does. Keeps on struggling, but in the shadows.'

Three amazing experiences.   Obviously, I moved carefully in Havana, for I was there to solve my personal problems, not to make waves or engage in contentious debate, but three more or less astonishing events were forced upon me and I profited, for they showed me a much different Cuba than I had expected. Masking names and locations regarding the first two, I affirm that these things happened as I describe them.

The first was a meeting with some two dozen cultural and in a sense political leaders, a gracious evening buffet at which the Cubans introduced a score of vital questions regarding our two nations, which I tried to answer forthrightly. In return, I questioned them about the cultural life in their country and their prospects for the future. It was as lively an interchange as I would have had at Harvard or Stanford when men and women of good intention and wide interest meet to hone their perceptions and broaden their understandings. There were limits, of course: I did not question them about Fidel Castro and Russia, they did not heckle me about Ronald Reagan and Nicaragua, but we did investigate a score of lesser problems. They remained staunchly Cuban and I just as resolutely American, but ideas flashed and held sway. It was the kind of evening that men and women on both sides would long remember. Both nations are the poorer that it is not endlessly repeated, for we do exist, whether we like it or not, rubbing elbows.

An important diplomat, learning that I was in Cuba if only briefly, arranged a quiet dinner attended by Spain's ambassador to Cuba, plus Monsignor Carlos Manuel de Céspedes, a leading luminary of Cuba's Catholic church. Here, in a less public gathering, no holds were barred. We spent some four hours in the most intense exchange of experiences and ideas; I felt privileged to learn how Spain regarded her former colony, the last she had been able to hold on to in the New World where her experience had once been so primordial and so powerful. And I think the ambassador may have been pleased to hear how highly I regarded his king and queen, who had proved so capable in helping convert their nation from a Franco dictatorship into a working democracy.

I was even more interested in ascertaining how Cuba had responded during three or four different periods to the power of the Catholic church. I told the very wise prelate: 'Like most American scholars who try to keep in touch with what happens in Cuba, I was of the opinion that in the worst days of the right-wing dictatorships your Church was seen by most outsiders as a handmaiden to repression, but that when a dictatorship of the left took power you became a beacon light for freedom. What an amazing transformation within a few years!' He added refinements to my simplistic analysis but then expressed considerable interest upon learning that I

had known Pope John Paul II while he was still an
embattled cardinal in Cracow and had visited him
several times since he attained the Vatican, and
would soon be visiting him again.

It was the kind of evening when ideas flowed
easily and constantly, with a few unexpected in-
sights revealing themselves now and then. I was impressed by the capacity of Spain to retain philosoph-
ical leadership in the New World, and the Church's
insistence upon retaining a foothold, however ten-
uous and however abused, in those bad years from
1960 through 1980. As the dignified prelate spoke,
so obviously a man of dedication and practical skill
as required by the political in-fighting, I thought of
the nuns in that back street providing the social assistance so critically needed in all societies, and I
thought: 'A powerful team, this one. Prelate in the
glare of the sun, nun in the merciful shadows.'

On Sunday night my hosts astonished me: 'Cuba's
finest pianist, a man with the unusual name of Frank
Fernández, highly regarded in Russia, Europe, and
South America, is giving a grand performance of
Beethoven concertos with Cuba's Orquesta Sin-
fónica Nacional. We have arranged seats for you and
John Kings, if you would like to join us.'

I had certainly not expected such a relaxing inter-
lude in what had to be a rushed working trip, but I
grabbed at the opportunity and was rewarded by a
memorable evening that had, as you will see, highly
personal overtones.

When Kings and I approached the concert hall
we were little prepared for what we were to see, for
he exclaimed several times: 'Look at these handsome people. Every man seems to have that one
good suit he wears on exceptional occasions, every
woman that elegant dress for the gala evening!' The
audience was indeed as resplendent as I would have
seen at a concert in Madrid, Munich, or San Fran-

cisco, and for some reason I could not have explained, then or now, I was quietly pleased that this was so. It was to be an important evening shared with important people.

It is difficult to define the excitement I experienced when I saw which of the five Beethoven piano concerti Maestro Fernández was offering that night: to open the concert, the noble Fifth, held by many to be the world's finest union of orchestra and piano, an honored war horse of the music halls that never fails to excite. I was surprised that it was to be played first, for most pianists save it for a triumphant and crashing climax.

Tonight the finale was to be the Fourth, a marvelous, dreamy understatement of exquisite organization and texture, and I was overjoyed to learn that it would be played, and for a reason that no one else in the hall would appreciate. I had that very month been writing an essay to be published at some time in the future explaining how my entire approach to writing my long novels like *Hawaii, The Source,* and *Alaska* had generated from my early appreciation back in 1929 of Beethoven's Piano Concerto No. 4 in G Major. What awed me then, when I already knew the bombastic concerti of Grieg, Schumann, and Tchaikovsky with their flamboyant openings, was the solemn, almost monotone manner in which Beethoven whispered the announcement that he was about to write a great concerto. Indeed, during long moments at the beginning the piano did not even participate, for he did not want it to run wild; he wanted it to slip in quietly at its proper place and then to enchant the hearer with its sublime music. General audiences do not like the Fourth with its muted beginning, but musicologists appreciate it for its mastery and rich significances. I adored it and said: 'If Beethoven can start his work slowly, and delay introducing his main themes till he's well along, I can do the same with my novels,' and it was this conviction that encouraged me to construct my novels the way I do, with long and patient preambles before the main actors appear. One critic properly said: 'It's fifty pages before we encounter any living thing and then it's a dinosaur. Ninety pages before any human being says a word.' Many readers quit my books early; those who hang on find themselves in carefully prepared worlds from which they are loath to depart.

In Havana that night I listened to Beethoven's Fifth with the delight that all audiences find in it, but when the Fourth began, I sank deep in my chair and allowed this gracious music, so deftly presented by the composer, so elegantly played by the pianist, to sweep over me, and I was again mesmerized by it; once more I was a student in my early twenties discovering one of the great secrets of art: 'You are free to begin slowly and build to meaningful climaxes. You're not obligated to attract attention with bugle calls.'

The highlight of the unexpected evening came when the management sent a messenger to our seats: 'The Maestro would be pleased if you would join him later in the Green Room,' and when we entered the kind of small, congenial room in which in auditoriums around the world performers meet with their friends at the conclusion of a concert or an opera or a play, I could have been in Tokyo or Leningrad, for the atmosphere of excitement and triumph and love of art was the same. When I thanked Maestro Fernández for having played the Fourth so elegantly, he said: 'It's a test for pianists, that one. To hold all things in balance. To help the listener to know a great piece of music,' and then he referred to Beethoven in one of the most powerful phrases I had ever heard applied to this great musician: 'el gran sordo de Bonn,' the grand deaf one of Bonn.

At the very moment he said this I had waiting on
my desk back in Miami a memorandum to Kings:
'John, please see if any of our libraries has a recording of Beethoven's Fourth Piano Concerto in G.
I need to refresh my mind as to the first movement.'
That I should have stumbled, a few days later in
Havana, upon a live performance of this concerto,
not a recording, would be interpreted by some as di-
vine intervention. I thought it a remarkable example
of good luck.

Seeking consumer goods in Cuba. As we went
down a side street something caught my eye, and I
cried: 'Hey! Let's look at that one,' and inside another
abandoned church we found a horde of women eagerly
pawing through a collection of dresses that someone

had got hold of, legally or otherwise, and was peddling from improvised racks.

For lunch Pablo Armando took us to La Bodeguita del Medio (The Little Storehouse in the Middle of the Block), a popular dive frequented by Hemingway in the 1940s. Its walls were covered with a squirrel's nest of graffiti supplied by decades of convivial patrons. Their scribblings were so copious and in a frenzied way so joyously artistic that they formed an endless Jackson Pollack. A trio of marvelously skilled musicians wandered through, and once they learned that I liked Cuban music, they gave an extensive concert with me joining in on some of the songs. But when I asked for a favorite, "Cu-cu-ru-cu-cu Paloma," they protested: 'Oh, Señor, that's a Mexican song,' so I said: 'Well then, give me your very best Cuban one,' and they proudly introduced me to one of their classics.

The principal shopping street, Galiano, was long famous for its elegant small shops and bustling big department stores. As in the days when my characters would have been young, it was crowded and I thought: 'Well, Communism certainly hasn't dampened trade,' but it soon became apparent that most of the women I saw were in a queue leading to a store for women's shoes. When I asked a woman in line what she was doing she said: 'If you see a line, you jump in. They've passed the word they have only three sizes, but that's alright because if they don't have my size I'll buy a pair anyway and sell them off to some friend.'

Leaving the women in Galiano, we turned a corner into a comparable street that many preferred, San Rafael, which I too found more lively. There we entered a store that Cuban women loved, Fin del Siglo—end of the century—founded sometime around the 1880s, and one glimpse of the mournful interior convinced me that I had made a dismal mistake. This noble store, once filled with goods from all corners of the world, now had a ground floor of perhaps three dozen individual counters, two-thirds of which were unattended because they had nothing whatever to sell, and those that had merchandise had only one item, often in short supply and limited sizes. A local citizen who was with me said: 'Don't let them tell you the American embargo accomplishes nothing. It's strangling the flow of our consumer goods.'

Already disheartened by what I had seen of the bleak and empty stores with which the people of Havana had to contend, I was appalled when an informant whispered: 'For the past six months, no toilet paper of any kind. No toothpaste, same time. No cosmetics for young women, not of any kind, for the past year and a half.' As the litany went on I felt sick for I recalled the limited fare at La Bodeguita:

the only meat a slab of greasy pork, the only vegetables a few carrots and fried plantains, a tired leg of
chicken, but plenty of rice and black beans, 'Moros
y Judíos' they called them, Moors and Jews. I
thought: 'How terribly wrong this is. Tons of fresh
vegetables available in Florida only half a day away
by barge.' From that time on I looked at the kindly
Cubans I met with new insight: 'How can they still
support a regime that offers them so little? How can
they be so kind to me when they know I'm the
American enemy who keeps the goods from coming
in?' And then I muttered: 'But Castro brought this
on himself and on his nation.' Then a nagging question crept forward: 'But did he have pressure from
us in making this terribly wrong decision?'

Exploring the former Brazilian Embassy. When
leaving or returning to the American Residency I had
to pass the ruined mansions of Cubanacán and one majestic building kept catching my eye. It was a huge
place of considerable though fading beauty recalling
the 1880s and I wanted to inspect it, but the roadway
leading to it was barred with a chain and a huge sign
warning strangers to stay clear. Fortunately, I learned
that it was one of the favorite haunts of Betsy Taylor,
the U.S. principal officer's delightful and knowledgeable wife, and she volunteered that it was the former
Brazilian Embassy, and that she would be pleased to
take me to look at it.

When we slid around the chain and walked up to
the house I encountered two workmen who were
cleaning up a mess of some kind, and I expected them
to throw me off the grounds, but when I told them: 'Yo
soy amigo de Cuba. Tengo un gran interés en su histo-
ria,' they showed eagerness to help, and soon I was in a

patio whose equal I had never seen. It was delineated on four sides by perhaps thirty magnificent columns, each of a radically different colored marble, with some in the twisted Solomonic variation. Despite the ruin, or perhaps because of it, this was a patio for dreaming.

The interior of the mansion, rapidly crumbling and soon to be a complete loss, was magnificent; for example, the grand dining room contained, high on its lofty walls, a painting on canvas running completely around the room, depicting Columbus in his various manifestations, and Kings cried: 'They ought to restore that, if only for the celebrations in 1992,' but alas, it was torn and savaged in too many parts. And so it was with everything in this once noble embassy. One of the workmen told me: 'Last year experts came from Brazil and said the place could be restored for one million dollars American, but when our people made actual estimates it turned out to be three million. The Brazilians decided to let it go.'

I had never before been involved in a building at that delicate moment when all hangs in the balance, live or die, and later when I was alone and far from the embassy's visual magic I thought: 'Castro's right. Let the dead past bury its dead. Get on with today's work,' but then I remembered the hundreds of workmen I had watched in Russia, experts in molding or even carving angels from plaster of paris and mixing antique paint combinations. Year after year they worked restoring imperial palaces bombed by Germany in World War II, for although the communists had fought the owners of those palaces to the death, they understood that the buildings were a vital part of Russian history and deserved restoration. Had I been Castro twenty years ago I would have saved this Brazilian Embassy as an honest if flamboyant echo of Cuban history. Now it's too late.

Visiting a marriage hall.   I was now ready to concentrate on my two big problems, the house and the plantation, but I had come to realize that what I really needed was two houses, so I asked Professor Otero: 'Where did my fictional family live in 1920? Where did they live in 1959? And where was their sugar plantation in whose ruins their descendants live today?' He replied: 'We'll leave the sugar mill till tomorrow. Let's look at the 1959 house first,' and he led me to a string of houses in an attractive area of the city where I spotted the kind of residence I sought. Piling out of our car after I shouted: 'Stop! That's it!' I climbed a slight hill to what I supposed would be a typical businessman's house, but a surprise awaited. It had indeed once belonged to a wealthy sugar baron, but Castro had expropriated it for a Hall of the People, which young couples could use, at little expense, for their weddings. The approach to the house attempted to establish the proper mood, with two handsome white marble nudes, but alas they were both females, a sym-

bolism I did not catch. Inside, things improved, for the ceiling of the marriage hall contained a fine mural of two nude lovers floating on diaphanous clouds, but one man in our group was pretty sure that the figure I took to be the man was really another woman, and I quit the argument there.

Instead, I followed an attractive young couple who had come with their friends for a wedding, which was conducted with propriety by a civil officer, not a clergyman. When the ceremony ended, a man whispered: 'How cruel. They get married at four in the afternoon, then enjoy a kind of honeymoon by walking around the garden out there, but then separate, he to his parents' home, she to hers, because it could be six or seven years before they'll be able to find a home of their own.'

Finding My House in El Cerro

ONE MORNING Otero said: 'I spent much of last night wondering where your 1920 house would have been, and I discarded quite a few possibilities because I understood your need for something distinctive and Cuban, but I failed to identify it. Then, at breakfast this morning, it came to me, a complete scenario. We're going to El Cerro.' I said: 'In all my reading I didn't discover that Havana had a hill,' which was what the word meant, and he chuckled: 'A slight rise . . . southwest of the old city . . . but deliciously cool in those years before air conditioning.'

As we drove in that direction he explained: 'At the close of the last century rich families had a big house in town and a spacious country-like residence in El Cerro, and they spent money like mad to make their summer homes works of art. Look as the main street comes at you!' and as I stared ahead I saw an architectural marvel: a moderately wide street lined with luxurious houses, each of which was fronted by a set of six or eight or ten handsome stone columns, like those before a Greek temple. The effect was almost mesmerizing, an endless colonnade in various materials and styles marching backward into the past.

But what added significance to the scene, and brought it within my story, was the fact that behind the lovely façades a number of the old mansions had fallen into total decay. Nothing existed but the shell and as I studied the mournful effect of six magnificent Greek columns hiding a mansion that no longer existed my learned guide explained in elegiac tones: 'The steps went down by decades. 1920s the

mansions are in full flower. 1930s the rich families begin to move out. 1940s people grab them who can't afford to maintain them, ruin begins. 1950s ten big families move into each mansion, pay no rent, and begin to tear it apart. 1960s during the first years of the revolution, no housing elsewhere, so even more crowd in, ruin accelerates. 1970s some of the weakest begin to fall down. 1980s many gone beyond salvation.' This was exactly the story I had wanted, not to tell but to imply, and as this tremendous visual impact struck, I stood dumbfounded, for it was so much more powerful than I had imagined.

The fighting swans of El Cerro.   But then a strange thing happened. As I walked down the street with the car trailing behind, I came upon the very house I wanted for my family in the 1920s, very Cuban, extraordinary to see, and not at all ruined. What set it apart was its façade decorated by some four dozen cast-iron swans, each standing tall and slim, its long neck bent straight down in mortal combat with an evil serpent climbing up its leg to sink its fangs. To see two score of these fantastically clever iron castings marching wing to wing and handsomely painted in bright colors was exciting.

My search for a house had ended: 'This is it!' I cried, for I could visualize my characters living there. I was so pleased with my discovery that I went to the unscarred door, banged upon it rather rudely, and watched it open to admit me to an adventure I could not have imagined. The Cuban who let me in was a tall, thin man in his fifties with a most engaging smile and naked to the waist. 'Soy norteamericano con un gran interés en su casa,' I said, and he reached for his shirt: 'Ay, mi madre, un norteamericano. ¡Venga, venga!' and he led me into a dark and solemn wonderland, rooms filled with cobwebs and ominous shadows and he always ahead, calling me to follow.

Slowly I began to see, in the darkness, that the ceiling of the first floor had been removed, and I supposed that this meant the house had fallen into ruin, all except the swan-filled portico. But then I saw looming from the shadows great casks, I mean oaken-staved casks fifteen and twenty feet high, with untold numbers of smaller ones stacked along the walls.

'Contraband?' I asked, and he replied sharply: '¡No! ¡No! La famosa Destilería Bocoy, ¡ron!' and that's what it was, a rum distillery belonging to one of the great firms but tucked away in this unlikely

spot because the rents were low or because the
Bocoy people had placed it here to serve their hard-
drinking customers in the 1890s. It was something
out of Piranesi, a ghostly affair with a single un-
shaded light bulb shining far in the distance, and
as we explored the deep recesses, my guide gave
me the ages of the various casks, their wood alone
worth a small fortune, and also the ages of their contents. It was an exploration I could not have imagined, but there was a keener surprise in store, for
when we reached the manager's office he excused
himself, then came back proudly, hands behind his
back. Almost awkwardly, but with obvious appreciation for the strange visit I had imposed upon him,
he brought forth his hands to produce a frail card-
board box in the shape of a pirate's treasure chest
and labeled La Isla del Tesoro (Treasure Island).
'¡Ábretele!' he cried as if he were my uncle at
Christmas, and when I did open it I found a large
bottle of one of the choicest rums distilled in Cuba.

'We make a little of this each year,' he said. 'Gifts
for important people like generals.' He laughed then
added: 'And today you're a general.'

Placid Experiences

ONE NIGHT as I lay in bed I said: 'Caution, Michener. For three days you've had nothing but the kindest possible reception from the Cuban people, not one of whom could have known who you were . . . just an American who knew a little Spanish and who had an interest in whatever they were doing. But that isn't the whole story. Remember the reports you've read about the horrible prison camps where men have been kept in torture conditions for whole decades. Abominable. Remember the reports you've received from our government about Castro's unwavering enmity toward us and the oral reports you've heard in your various jobs in Washington. This is enemy territory. Maintain a balance.'

The next day was filled with those placid experiences that, interspersed with those of dramatic meaning, produce so much pleasure for the traveler. We were driving down another narrow street when I asked for a halt, and we went unannounced into a vast former monastery or convent; I was told which but I forget. It was under reconstruction, a costly undertaking, for its size was so stupendous that I could not imagine how it would be used when renovated. It had not one central patio, but three, the first much larger, it seemed to me, than a football field, with a bleak, bare church attached that could hold a thousand if restored. It had been used, I was told, as a storage barn for grain, but I could not ascertain to what use it would be put in the future, for there were no indications that it would ever revert to being a church. Regardless of its ultimate destiny, I was glad to see that a notable old building would see new life.

Paying respects to a Cuban novelist.   When I was
asked: 'Whom would you like to meet in Havana?' I
naturally replied: 'Castro' but was told 'Impossible.
Who else?' and I said: 'You have a very fine novelist here, Alejo Carpentier, and I'd like to pay my
respects.'

'He died some years ago, but there's a little museum
commemorating him and his work,' so off we went to
visit a handsome shrine that bespoke his fiery spirit.
Carpentier, last name pronounced in the French style,
was a gifted writer who fled Cuba in the bad days of
the Batista dictatorship to live in Venezuela, where he
continued to write novels that were amazingly erudite
and verbally explosive. When the Castro revolution
succeeded, he hurried back to Cuba as an honored artistic and spiritual leader.

In my travels about the Caribbean I had often heard
him praised by pro-communists, decried by anti's, but
since I had read none of his work I could form no opinion of my own; however, a curious accident moved me
into intimate contact. I was researching my novel in
Guadeloupe, trying unsuccessfully to uncover information about a murderous rascal, one Victor Hugues,
who during the height of the French Revolution lugged
a personal guillotine onto the island and used it hor-
ribly. Disconsolate about my failure, I was brooding
when a Frenchman told me: 'The Cuban novelist Carpentier has an entire novel on Hugues; *Explosion
in a Cathedral* is the title in English. You'll find it
rewarding.'

I did, and I appreciated the book so much that I
wanted to see the house the author had featured in it
and to catch, perhaps, some glimmer of what he
himself might have been like. The little museum
was a gem, a central courtyard of considerable
beauty surrounded by the rooms in which Carpentier had worked. One entire wall, not lengthy, was
dedicated to a display under sloping glass of his

principal works, including an early printing of the
novel that had meant so much to me. My version of
the mass murderer Hugues was going to be radically different from his, but I respected the considerable work he had done in ferreting out the man's
history. The book had been written in exile in 1956,
published first in Mexico, in Spanish, and given
wide attention in a French version in 1962, which is
usually cited as the date of origin. It appeared in a
fine English translation as a Penguin Classic in
1963 and has enjoyed wide acceptance ever since in
those three languages. From the museum one gets a
strong sense of the working novelist and a revolu-
tionary patriot, for he held important cultural posi-
tions in the Castro government.

The museum was of special interest to me in that
it is the work of Carpentier's widow, who has applied his posthumous royalties to keep his memory
alive, and she has succeeded. It's a small museum,
remember, the display area limited to only one room
really, but it sings of Cuba and of love.

Paying respects to an American novelist. From
there we motored well out into the country to the east
of Havana to pay homage to a much different kind of
writer memorialized in a much different kind of museum. La Vigía, the country home in which Ernest
Hemingway lived during his productive stays in Cuba,
sits within a spacious finca, a landed estate imposing in
design, elevation, and appearance. It is a masterpiece,
really, and a portrait of the vital writer who occupied
it. The house is a well-constructed, open tropical home
of interlocking rooms generously spaced and is maintained as if the owner had a few minutes ago driven
into Havana to meet with friends at La Bodeguita del
Medio. Into whatever room one wanders, there one
finds the ghost of Hemingway: at his desk working, in
bed reading magazines, in his dressing room trying to

decide which of sixteen pairs of shoes he will wear, in
a retreat listening to classical music on an intricate
sound system, in a trophy room guarded by African
animals, or in his living room with its huge poster an-
nouncing a forthcoming bullfight featuring Domingo
Ortega as matador.

The house, carefully tended by a trained curator,
Sra. Gladys Rodríguez, is a treasure, crammed in
every available corner with the huge number of
books he collected on the widest spread of interest.
Books grow old quickly in this climate with no protection against humidity and insects, and one won-

ders if there is any sense in trying to maintain so many when protection is so costly. They are impressive, no doubt about it, but could their titles not be placed in a computer system from which their variety could be studied?

The grounds of La Vigía are as interesting as the house and as evocative of Hemingway: a huge swimming pool, a high square tower that is an apartment to itself, guest house, garage, tennis court, and awesome in its size, his famous boat *Pilar*, within a monstrous steel-girder construction that must have cost thousands of dollars. I had the sorrowful feeling that the good people struggling to keep the huge complex alive were attempting too much, by a large margin. All parts may soon start to deteriorate, and in the tropics ruin comes swiftly, but I am not wise enough to advise what ought to be maintained or how.

Jerry Scott, my guide, is a devoted Hemingway buff and has a host of sensible ideas: 'Imagine what will happen if tour ships ever come back to Havana! Each will feature a ride through the countryside out to the Hemingway museum, two bucks a head, we could harvest a fortune.' Then he strokes his beard: 'When you think of the prices brought at the Andy Warhol auction, can you imagine what the contents of this Hemingway house would bring? His rifles. His African boots. His annotated books. His bullfight posters. His writing desk. His chairs. His fishing boat. We're guarding a fortune here, and if relations between our countries ever become normal, every self-respecting American or European or Asian tourist will have to come out here to see where the great man lived, and how.' He then said with sadness: 'I would like to find a way to keep the place in decent condition until Castro is gone and Americans will be able to enjoy it. Hemingway deserves that much from his friends.'

Coffee or Sugar?

NEXT DAY SCOTT arranged a caravan to head out to my final target, and for this we had the expert guidance of Professor Manuel Moreno Fraginals, author of a world-famous three-volume history of the Cuban sugar industry. In working with these learned men of Cuba, and some of them like Fraginals are learned indeed, I noticed a distinction. In the States we refer to 'a professor from Cornell' or 'a distinguished professor from Bryn Mawr,' but in Cuba it was simply 'this notable professor of medicine,' and one never knew what his academic affiliation was or even if he had one. At the start he surprised me by saying: 'We'll be heading out to a fine sugar operation in Artemisa, a town well west of here, and there you'll find just what you want. Complete sugar plant in operation, mill and all, but I have a suspicion that what you really want, although you may not know it, is a wonderful old coffee plantation that went out of operation about 1910.'

I was irritated by what seemed an irrational deviation from the common-sense plan we had agreed upon. I wanted to see a sugar plantation and Moreno Fraginals was a world expert, so why waste his time and mine? But he was obdurate, leading me to the stately ruins of a once-powerful coffee plantation tucked west of Havana. To reach it, we turned south from the main road and traveled some distance along a flat dirt road lined here and there with trees. It led to an astonishing sight: a white marble statue of the Greek goddess of fertility, Artemis, guarding the ruins of an early-nineteenth-century mansion built when Spain still owned the island. It

was stupendous in size, with all four walls still standing but beginning to crumble. The roof was gone, even the frames of the windows were knocked out, and a vast loneliness reigned. I sat among the ruins, trying to imagine what life must have been like in such a palace. I could see a grizzled veteran of the coffee wars living here, fighting off the nagging government agents sent out from Madrid, a sorry lot, and no doubt sharing his mansion with five or six of his children and their families. They must have had at least thirty servants for the mansion alone, a hundred for the grounds, and up to six hundred slaves hidden away somewhere.

I could have spent three days in this haven of a past era; because of my writing in Spain I could appreciate the forces that operated in such a planta-

tion, but even so I was in for some powerful shocks, for at this point I had seen only the living quarters. When I left the ruins and followed a streamlet to a much lower level, I found myself in a collection of five or six gigantic subterranean cisterns into which the copious supplies of water required in handling coffee beans were collected; it was like a scene from Dante. But it was when I climbed out of the cisterns and onto the plateau above that I came upon the salient fact of this great operation: the immense fenced-in area in which the slaves were kept, an area so vast that five or six football fields could have been fitted in. One look at it told you what you needed to know about the growing of coffee. The mournful place, called a *barracón*, had only one gate, beside which rose a tall stone tower in which men with

guns waited day and night for any sign of incipient rebellion. I thought, as I took notes in this forgotten corner of a coffee plantation that probably shifted to sugar some time around the turn of the century: 'You did a good job in your bookish study of these matters. You got the details right, all those treatises from the library. But the heart of the matter you missed entirely. You did not catch the immensity of the mansion, the ghostly quality of the cisterns, the cruel sternness of that armed tower, the awful gravity of that *barracón* with its iron gate. It was worth two years of fruitless effort to get here, for writing can never reverberate with meaning if the essential images are lacking.'

Finding my plantation. But I was still lacking my sugar plantation and mill, and since modern Cuba pretty much exists on sugar—and has done so for most of this past century—I deemed it essential that I see that operation. 'We'll be going to Artemisa,' Moreno Fraginals said, 'an excellent example of the way we do things today,' and when we reached this lovely rural town I found all the images I had sought. Here were the rolling green fields rich with the ripening sugarcane, the rude pathways along which tractors hauled the cane to the mill, the huge buildings where the cane was crushed, and the dozen or so other buildings in which the hard work of making sugar was conducted. The mill was not working, of course, for its season for grinding pulp would start after the New Year, but scores of mechanics were repairing machinery against the time when it would be running twenty-four hours a day, and I was astonished by how much heavy gear was required to reduce a length of succulent greenish cane into a spoonful of white sugar. This was the heart of Cuba, for as sugar went, so went the Cuban economy. Explained one of the workmen: 'If the Soviet Union stopped buying our sugar at three cents above the world price, we'd be in sore trouble.'

Since I had once worked in Greeley, Colorado, a short distance from a beet-sugar mill and knew the process, and the healthful, earthy smell of sugar extraction, I asked: 'What do you men in Cuba do with your bagasse?' I was speaking of the fibrous pulp that is left after the sugar juices have been squeezed out, and they said: 'We're trying to make many things from it . . . fiber board . . . imitation wood.' When I asked if they fed it to their animals, they laughed at the idea and I explained that with sugar beets—a product anathema in the Caribbean since such beets, easily grown, harvested, and processed in states like Colorado, have almost destroyed the wealth the islands used to garner from their

cane—we mixed the dry pulp with the molasses re-
sulting from the refining procedure to make one of
the world's finest foods for cattle: 'The steers you see
in cowboy movies, all fed on sugar-beet bagasse.'
They thought this so remarkable that I forgot to
ask them if cattle would also eat cane bagasse. As
before, the workmen were almost glad to see an
American, and I enjoyed a thorough conversation
on sugar matters with a fine looking fellow in blue
work clothes who seemed to be the manager. But
when I asked him at the end of our visit if we could
photograph him, he hastily called an older man to
ask if it would be permitted, and I judged that this
fellow, who had seemed so inconspicuous during
our visit, was the party leader. He studied me for
some moments, looked uneasily at the camera, then
said with a restrained smile: '¿Porqué no?' (Why
not?) and both Kings and Scott took a series of shots.

While I was talking further with the managers,
Kings had found one of the highlights of our visit, a
very black workman with a very large belly and no
shirt hiding it. He turned out to be a jovial Sancho
Panza eager to gossip in his robust way about the
sugar industry, of which he had always been a part.
His humor was infectious and his use of hands so artistic as he moved them about to make his points
that I felt it a privilege to be with him, and he in
turn took a liking to his inquisitive American.
When I asked him his name he told me proudly, and
then asked mine. I was about to give him the correct
answer, 'Jaime' when I thought it would be more
appropriate to the setting to use the old Biblical
equivalent of James: 'Yo soy Santiago.' This pleased
him for it made me one of his group, and when I
finally pulled away from the mill, overpowered by
the images I had collected, he ran after the car
shouting one of the warmest farewells I've ever had:
'Hasta la vista mi amigo Santiago.'

Brainse Carman Cloch
Dolphin's Barn Branch
Tel: 540681

It was a sad and disappointing departure, for although the men at the sugar plantation had been most helpful, I had realized as we talked that there was no way I could fit their huge, brooding, metallic structure into my story. The images were too alien. But that accidental coffee plantation! On its ruins one could write a score of chapters. As so often happens with all artists, I had not known what I was seeking till I found it.

A press conference and a revelation. I was in
Havana for only six days and saw nothing that would
entitle me to generalize about the politics, the dictatorial repressions, or the near-term relationship between Cuba and the United States. I saw little of the
hinterland and nothing of the eastern end of the island,
but I did see the things I sought: the houses and the
plantation, and what turbulent, mind-agitating images
they provided.

I remember two other things. In Havana I saw
hordes of the most enchanting children, all in regi-
mented school uniforms so colorful they looked like a
meadow of flowers. Well nourished, well shod and
clothed, they were the permanent face of the land. And

with a daring that surprised me, Jerry Scott circulated word that on the evening before I was to leave on the 2:00 A.M. plane there would be a press conference at which I would try to answer questions thrown at me.

We approached the affair nervously, because we could not know if any newspeople would come, or be allowed by the government to come, but when I entered Scott's apartment I found about two dozen sharp, knowledgeable young reporters from the various media, Cuban, European, and even a Pole, ready to tear into me. We talked for two hours, some of the most perceptive discussions I've had, and after even those who came to give me hell saw that I really would answer their questions with whatever intelligence and openness I commanded, they began to invite me to question them. At the end of two hours none of us wanted to part.

They told me: 'This is the first serious conference like this we've had with an American in years. It was a privilege.' I told them: 'Shuttle planes ought to be leaving Miami and Havana each day. You need us and we need you. I hope it can be worked out before the end of the century with each nation satisfied that it has protected its own interests.' And one of them whispered as we parted: 'You can't guess how nervous we are these days. What will happen if glasnost really catches on in the Soviet Union and they pull back from their overseas adventures? Where will that leave us?' and I thought: 'Where indeed?'

With that I left for my almost-secret night flight, and only thirty-eight minutes later I was in Miami, thinking: 'So near, and yet such worlds apart!' But I was content. I had captured my images, brought them home, and could now use them to finish my manuscript.

A few days later, Miami papers reported that security police had arrested nine dissident Cubans. Their crime? They had organized a public homage to Cuba's

great patriot, José Martí, at which they demanded
more freedom of expression for artists and writers. In
response the government activated strenuous counter-
measures against any artists guilty of 'deviationist
works.' The repression was encouraged by Politburo
member José Marchado Ventura, who called for harsh
sanctions against those arrested, condemning them
as 'anti-socials.' What will happen to them in prison,
I cannot guess.

In Havana
by John Kings

In Havana

by John Kings

THE LEAST IMPORTANT item I packed for our visit to Cuba was a camera. Normally for a research field trip I would take a bulky camera with a long lens, a wide angle, and one for close-up work including the copying of documents, old photographs, etc. to which James Michener might want to refer later. We had no set rules for this photographic coverage and I was normally guided only by what I felt might be of some use later. The idea was to make a record, not in any way a statement, and the method had worked well for many journeys since first working on *Centennial*.

But the parameters for the Cuba journey were very different. I was warned that photography was generally frowned upon in Castro's embattled isle, that it would be imprudent, to say the least, to wander about with obviously professional equipment strung around my neck, and generally that I would be asking for trouble if I took my usual, though modest, assortment of gear. So I decided to leave it behind. Apart from any other consideration the shutter of my Nikon sounds like the closing of a steel trap. It can be heard clear across a crowded room and I had visions of heavily armed men running to frustrate my innocent purposes. I had no wish to be interrogated, not because I had any evil intent to conceal, but rather because it would be time wasted in an already too-short trip. So it took no second thoughts for me not to take that equipment.

Instead, I took a very compact West German rangefinder 35-mm camera called a Balda CA 35 with a sharp f2.8/38-mm lens and a shutter click soft as a whisper. I left behind the flash attachment for the same reason that I left behind the big Nikon. Altogether too attention-getting. Convinced that there would be little occasion even to use this small camera I included only three rolls of film, an unheard of small amount when venturing into unknown territory, but proof indeed that photography was at the bottom of my list of expectations for this trip.

The rest of the story is obvious from this book. From the moment I arrived my eyes registered image upon image that I wanted to record. I exhausted the three rolls within the first two hours of being in the old city, and, even more surprising, nobody objected, no one was following us, there were no street-corner cadres of soldiers scanning the scene for photographers; my cautious advisers in Miami had been very wide of the mark. Now my only fear was that I would not be able to buy more film.

I was wrong. A helpful member of our little party immediately offered to take me to a nearby store and within minutes I was able to lay in a stock of Kodak and Fuji film, rolls and rolls of it, at a cost comparable to what I was used to paying in Miami. I was excited beyond measure. Now I could take photographs virtually at will in what was obviously one of the most photogenic cities in the world.

Havana is a photographer's dream of light and shadows, of cluttered streets and houses, of bright and faded colors, of the very old and the not so new, of broad vistas of avenue and ocean, of contrasts of decrepitude and elegant restoration, and of the flow of people on their daily rounds. It was captivating and challenging and for the next five days my finger barely left the shutter of my little German eye.

My only limitations were the short span of our visit and the demands of our research. Wherever Michener's acute sense of place and people took him I followed and shot the scene. There would be no

second chances, so I took photographs in rain and
shine, in early morning and late evening, inside and
outside, never able to go back for a retake or choose
a certain time of day or compose a group. As
Michener walked so I walked, often wanting to re-
trace my steps for one more shot of a scene, but always aware that I might miss out on the next object
of his attention. It was all immediate and un-
premeditated. Together we caught Havana just as it
was in those six days, with never a trick to empha-
size or distort a subject.

I may go back again one day, but it will never be
with the same feelings of exhilaration and utter surprise that this first visit engendered. And if I do return in happier times, I believe I may yet again leave
behind all my equipment except the little Balda
CA 35.

Vista de la Plaza vieja ó Mercado Principal de la Habana.

The Old City

THE OLD SPANISH colonial city of Havana anchors the whole capital. Much has grown round it in the centuries since it was the jewel of New Spain, but no later development has reduced its prominence and lure. Across the river from Morro Castle, the courtyards of its noble houses, the hush and cool of its great cathedral, its broad plazas fed by arteries of narrow cobbled streets all conjure more a vision of a rich colonial past than any link with the Communist present. And yet it is an important visual link with the past, and widely recognized as such by the present government. Aided by funds from Spain and from UNESCO, ambitious restoration is under way, to the walled convents and palaces, to the surrounding houses that epitomize the living styles and habits of the rich and poor, and to the bastion fortress of De la Fuerza, now landlocked but formerly commanding the sea which lapped against its towering walls.

The old city is a rich mixture of enchanting colonial Spanish architecture, with a grace and style equaled in the whole Caribbean only by the magnificence of the great walled city of Cartagena. Its doorways and arches and frescoes, its balconies and columns and courtyards combine in a glorious artistic expression that is all grace and elegance. Nothing that could be done with stone and chisel has been omitted. Little wonder that this area is now a rich drawing card for tourists from eastern bloc countries. How wise of Fidel Castro not to erase it in the name of proletarian progress.

The old city is a vivid reminder of a great imperial power in the New World. Spain's colonial license eventually expired, but the grandeur of old Havana lives on. Cuba is richer for its continuing presence, and we soon became prisoners of its charm and allure.

The Gilded Age

FOLLOWING SPAIN'S dominance of Cuba, at the conclusion of the brief Spanish-American War in 1898, a new age of elegance brought the addition of big hotels, swanky yacht clubs, department stores, casinos, and lavish restaurants in an almost unlimited outpouring of American capital. Soon Havana became a Mecca for the well-heeled of three continents—North and South America and Europe—its fleshly attractions beckoning the bored and indolent to yet another playground.

Fine parks and monuments to generals and patriots were added, the broad Malecón promenade handsomely contained the long waterfront, bandstands and open-air cafés catered to the strolling throng. Havana's harbor bobbed with gilded yachts and opulent liners, its opera house echoed to the great voices of Paris, London, and Milan, its theatres rang curtain call after curtain call to the leading actors and actresses of the world stage.

But wealth also accounted for architectural vulgarity. The main cemetery is itself an exercise in pious excesses almost beyond belief. In death as in life the wealthy vied for immortality in monumental dimension. Havana attracted the best and the worst in about the same proportion. If it became known disenchantingly as the whorehouse of America, it also earned a reputation as the Paris of the Caribbean. Either way it was a colorful and sensual city. My brother-in-law told me that in 1946 he visited Havana aboard the *USS Princeton,* then one of the Navy's largest carriers. 'We could smell Havana when we were still many, many miles away. The

mixed aroma of coffee, tobacco, sugar and rum was so strong that I can smell it still. And when we entered the narrow passage between the city and Morro Castle the water around us was jammed with rowboats full of clamoring prostitutes!'

In one guise or another licentious Havana persisted for sixty years or so, until the course of history again changed its face. Today the Russian submarines that nose quietly into the harbor enjoy no such welcome as was extended to my brother-in-law. The city is squarely puritan and even that distinctive and cloying aroma is no longer borne seaward on the offshore breeze.

Faded Glory

THERE ARE SEVERAL immediate impressions of the city of Havana today. It is, indeed, generally decrepit and badly needs a face lift. But joy of joys, there is no graffiti defacing the walls, except for occasional government slogans, there are no parking meters, no litter, there are no beggars or vagrants, no molestation, and it is safe for women to walk alone. Traffic is in about the right proportion for a city, albeit because of a chronic shortage of vehicles, and driving is of the highest standard I have found anywhere in the Caribbean, due to the very difficult driving test which itself keeps many people off the roads. And nobody is smoking cigars.

This latter surprised me. In six days I saw a total of five people smoking cigars. Perhaps like Scotch in the lean days of Britain after WW II, the main production goes overseas to earn much-needed currency. Whatever the reason it came as a shock, though the embers of remembrance of my *Romeo & Juliet* cigars were pleasantly rekindled when I was able to buy a small tin of them to take back to Miami. The odd rule of U.S. Customs is that if you are permitted to go to Cuba, you are also permitted to bring back a reasonable quantity of Cuban cigars. What is forbidden is that you bring them back to the United States from any country other than Cuba.

If you don't have to live in it the rampant dilapidation in every part of Havana almost has its own sad charm. With an acute shortage of housing, every building and structure that has the slightest chance of holding together is put to habitable use. Behind crumbling façades festooned with makeshift

wiring, inside tottering buildings that long ago should have faced the bulldozer's maw, Cubans cling to a semblance of family life in a fashion that displays their ingenuity and tenacity.

The streets of the city throng with clean, good-looking, brightly clad people. Any commodity you can name is likely to be in short supply for weeks, months, or even years, but somehow the housewives find soap for washday. 'Cubans are very clean people,' I was told. 'To take away their soap would be Castro's greatest folly. Almost anything else can be tolerated but take away their soap and the regime would fall!' It seems that life is bearable as long as the clotheslines are swaying on every balcony in sight.

Laden with books and satchels, bright-eyed children wend their way to school wearing pin-neat uniforms colored according to their grades—red for elementary-age students, saffron for high school. Never did I see a neglected child, but behind peeling, broken shutters and the cracked panes of shabbily curtained windows the only things that make the privation bearable are the assurances of jobs, good medical services, and adequate food. Frills are not a part of the average Cuban's life in Havana, and perhaps only the kindness of the climate prevents the smoldering of revolt that might accompany the same conditions in a cold and relentless climate. Communism in the sun allows parameters that probably would not be tolerated in Eastern Europe and Russia.

But the sun does shine most of the time, the night air blows softly from the ocean, and people laugh and shout in the daily bustle of living. From the doorways and balconies comes the sassy beat of Cuban music and the voices of the lovelorn raised in song. There is nothing depressing about the people, only the manner in which they have to live.

Street Life Today

THE MAKESHIFT ENTERPRISES of street vendors in Havana are certain proof that capitalism is not dead in Cuba. On Saturday mornings the main plaza in the old city is thronged with crowds testing the wares of a widely diversified bunch of entrepreneurs. Need a new truss for your hernia? It's here. A trinket, a necklace, a bag, a game of chance? A hand of bananas, your photograph taken? It's all here gaudily displayed like a traveling show. Craftsmen with wood carvings or leatherwork jostle con men and balloon vendors, stocky tourists from eastern bloc countries snap a scene impossible to equal back home and return to their tourist hotels wide-eyed at the verve of their Cuban Communist cousins. Cuban *chutzpah* is as alive and well in Havana as it is in Miami.

In the streets Cubans are friendly and talkative to Americans, whom they seem to prefer to the Russians who supplanted them. Wherever we went, always informal and unannounced, we were greeted by total strangers with smiles and good manners. And by the time our visit was ended we felt we were leaving behind friends we would like to meet again. In no way could we condone the intolerant expressions of the regime, but we could surely feel warmth from our exposure to the many everyday Cubans we met in our six days in Havana.

Over and over again I had the feeling that the Cuban is a being apart, colorful, enterprising, and chock-full of verve, that regimes may come and go in different guises, but the essential Cuban will remain the same.

Cubans

TO TRAVEL THROUGH the islands of the Caribbean is a rich ethnic experience unmatched in other island groups around the world. The blending of cultures of four or five immensely different European nations, England, Spain, France, Holland, and Denmark, co-mingled with the African and to a lesser extent East Indian presence, plus the strains of the original Carib and Arawak native population, has led through the centuries to an immensely rich diversity among the islanders. There was one common denominator, sugarcane, and there is now another, tourism, but that's about it. The islands tend to go their own way based on their historical experience, they seem unable to forge either political or economic associations of consequence within the area, they are indeed like a fleet of oddly assorted vessels afloat in the Caribbean Sea.

Of these vessels, the largest by far is Cuba, and it, too, differs dramatically from its sister 'ships.' On this brief visit I was very aware that it is a multiracial society, with skin color from rich black to the palest shade of white. That in itself is not unlike many other Caribbean islands.

But the Cubans are different in one particular characteristic. They seem to possess a northern work ethic and drive combined with a southern joy of living that makes them unique. How it worked out that way is something I have been trying to determine for the last three years here in Miami. All I know for sure is that it's there and that it's formidable. The photographs which follow, of Cubans in Havana, speak clearly for themselves.

America in Cuba

THE NINETY MILES OF WATER separating Cuba from the southern tip of the United States is at present the widest and deepest moat in the world, a political chasm. But what of America in Cuba today? Is there a presence, albeit clandestine or subversive? The answer is a clear 'Yes' and its manifestations are remarkably overt. People line up to see American movies, every park and sandlot is alive with the clack of baseball on bat, however rudely fashioned both may be, the Western Union offices are open for business, and there is an acutely felt shortage of chewing gum. Those fortunate enough to own a TV can pick up mainland stations and share the network offerings of America. Most noticeable of all, the streets and roads boast a galaxy of old American cars that would gladden a vintage enthusiast's heart. It's as if time had stood still from the 50's, though the machines themselves bear the unmistakable signs of extensive wear. 'There's an Edsel that would be worth thousands and thousands in the U.S.,' a companion shouted as a medley of classic models swept by in the morning traffic. 'Look at those fins, catch that chrome,' as a glorious capitalist automobile at a traffic light nudged out a drab gray modern Lada from Russia. Those who have not inherited by some means or another one of those showy American behemoths will probably have opted for the motorbikes and sidecars into which every member of the family is crammed for weekend jaunts. Yes, Havana is a motor show with an undeniable American stamp on it.

Are there any American heroes left in Castro's

Cuba? Two spring immediately to mind, one American by extension, the other in many ways America's true American. The first, of course, is José Canseco, Cuban-born but now the Oakland A's star baseball player. Any visiting American is sure to be asked what Canseco's doing, children chant his name as they step up to bat, and he is their hero not only because he is Cuban but no doubt because he shows Yankee Americans just how the game should be played. In a sense Canseco hits home runs clear across the moat, and that's no bad thing.

The other hero, loved, revered, and whose memory is cherished, is Ernest Hemingway. There is a monument to him at the fishing village of Cohima, the setting for his novel *The Old Man and the Sea*. He wrote the first three chapters of *For Whom the Bell Tolls* in his workroom at the Hotel Ambos Mundos close by the old city of Havana, and his house, La Vigía, is preserved by the Castro government as a museum to his life and work.

Hemingway is an American with whom Cubans proudly and openly identify. No one has scrawled anti-American slogans on his monument, no one has toppled the gilded bust that crowns the monument. On weekends Cuban families throng to his home to relive the worldly adventures of their hero, to peer at his books and trophies, to view his beloved boat *Pilar* and to picnic endlessly in the spacious grounds of his estate. The memories of Ernest Hemingway are a strong tie for Cubans, at least to Key West and Florida, his favored mainland watering holes.

The unspoken ties between the two countries are many, not least in the thousands of families who have relatives now living in the United States. The blood of kinship links the two countries, just as the blood of political conflict still separates them.

Brainse Carnan Cloch
Dolphin's Barn Branch
Tel: 540681